_____

T o

_____

F r o m

_____

D a t e

THE FRUIT OF THE SPIRIT IS

Kindness

HONOR BOOKS
Tulsa, Oklahoma

Unless otherwise indicated, all Scripture quotations are taken from *The Holy Bible, New International Version* ®, NIV®. Copyright © 1973, 1978, 1984 by International Bible Society. Used by permission of Zondervan Publishing House. All rights reserved.

Scripture quotations marked as KJV, are taken from the *King James Version* of the Bible.

The Fruit if the Spirit is KINDNESS
ISBN # 1-56292-657-8
Copyright © 2000 by Honor Books
P.O. Box 55388
Tulsa, Oklahoma 74155

Compiled and edited by Paul M. Miller.

All possible efforts were made by Honor Books to secure permission and ensure proper credit given for every entry within this book.

LOVE IS KIND

Jesus replied,

"'Love the Lord your God with all your heart

and with all your soul

and with all your mind.'

This is the first and greatest commandment.

And the second is like it:

'Love your neighbor as yourself.'"

—MATTHEW 22:37-39

A BUSHEL OF Kindness

"Honey, what's an eight-letter word that's a 'fruit of the Spirit'?"

"That's easy. Here's a hint; think of a bumper sticker we saw."

"Bumper sticker?"

"Remember? 'Random Acts of . . .'"

"The Apostles?"

"A fruit of the Spirit!"

"Kumquats?"

"Check Galatians 5:22."

"How about Patience?"

"Good guess, but no. Look, it has to end in n-e-s-s."

"That's easy, 'Goodness.' Right?"

"Nope. This fruit is a result of 'Patience' and 'Goodness.'"

"Hmmm, then it has to be 'Kindness'!"

"Bingo!"

A fruit tree that is planted near a nourishing stream is more likely to bear choice fruit. Refreshing water helps the tree to bear good fruit. It's a natural process. Like the tree, when we fill our hearts with love and goodness, we can share the gift of kindness with others.

—PAUL M. MILLER

If you want to lift yourself up, lift up someone else.

—BOOKER T. WASHINGTON

No act of Kindness, no matter how small, is ever wasted.

—AESOP

Thou art a God ready to pardon, gracious and merciful,

slow to anger, and of great kindness.

—NEHEMIAH 9:17 KJV

Do not feel badly if your kindness is rewarded
with ingratitude; it is better to fall from your
dream clouds than from a third-story window.

—JOAQUIM MARIA MACHADO
DE ASSIS

To err is human, to forgive, divine.

—ALEXANDER POPE

Kindness is the oil that takes the friction.

—ANONYMOUS

If you were paid ten cents for every
kind word you ever spoke, and had to
pay out five cents for every unkind
word, would you be rich or poor?

—ANONYMOUS

When you are dog-tired at night,
could it be from growling all day long?

—ANONYMOUS

Shall we make a new rule of life from tonight:
always to try to be a little kinder than is necessary?

—J. M. BARRIE

A great many people do many things that seem to
be inspired more by a spirit of ostentation than by
heartfelt kindness. . . . Such a pose is nearer akin to
hypocrisy than to generosity or moral goodness.

—CICERO

True kindness presupposes the faculty of imagining
as one's own the sufferings and joy of others.

—ANDRE GIDE

Practice Random Kindness and Senseless Acts of Beauty.

—ANNE HERBERT
& MARGARET PAVEL

Kindness can become its own motive.

We are made kind by being kind.

—ERIC HOFFER

GOD'S LOVE FOR ISRAEL

I led them with cords of human
kindness, with ties of love;

I lifted the yoke from their neck
and bent down to feed them.

—HOSEA 11:4

I will tell of the kindnesses of the LORD,
the deeds for which he is to be praised,
according to all the LORD has done for us—
yes, the many good things he has done
for the house of Israel, according to
his compassion and many kindnesses.

–ISAIAH 63:7

Deeds of kindness are equal in weight to
all the commandments.

—T A L M U D

Throughout this toilsome world, alas!
Once and only once I pass;
If a kindness I may show,
If a good deed I may do
To a suffering fellow man,
Let me do it while I can.
No delay, for it is plain
I shall not pass this way again.

—ANONYMOUS

❧

Kindness Begets Kindness.

—SWEDISH SAYING

It is the experience of touching the pain of others that is the key to change. . . . Compassion is a sign of transformation.

—JIM WALLIS

The measure of love is compassion; the measure
of compassion is kindness.

—ANONYMOUS

THE APOSTLE PAUL ON KINDNESS

Be kindly affectioned one to another with brotherly love.

—ROMANS 12:10 KJV

A great man shows his greatness by the
way he treats little men.

—THOMAS CARLYLE

Kindly words do not enter so deeply
into men as a reputation for kindness.

—MENCIUS

What wisdom can you find that is greater than kindness?

—JEAN JACQUES ROUSSEAU

That best portion of a good man's life,

His little, nameless, unremembered acts

Of kindness and of love.

—WILLIAM WORDSWORTH

When I see a deed of kindness,
I am eager to be kind.
When a weaker brother stumbles
and a strong man stays behind
Just to see if he can help him,
then the wish grows strong in me
To become as big and thoughtful
as I know that friend to be.
And all the travelers can witness
that the best of guides today
Is not the one who tells them,
but the one who shows the way.

—EDGAR A. GUEST,
from *Sermons We See*

Kindness begets kindness evermore,

But he from whose mind fades the memory

Of benefits, noble is he no more.

—SOPHOCLES

Do a deed of simple kindness;

Though its end you may not see,

It may reach, like widening ripples,

Down a long eternity.

—JOSEPH NORRIS
from *Influence*

❧

"With everlasting kindness I will have compassion on
you," says the LORD your Redeemer.

—ISAIAH 54:8

In this world, you must be a bit too kind
in order to be kind enough.

—PIERRE MARIVAUX

Consider therefore the kindness and
sternness of God: sternness to those
who fell, but kindness to you, provided
that you continue in his kindness.

—ROMANS 11:22

Kind words can be short and easy to
speak, but their echoes are truly endless.

—MOTHER TERESA

As God's chosen people, holy and dearly loved,
clothe yourselves with compassion, kindness,
humility, gentleness and patience.

—COLOSSIANS 3:12

We cannot tell the precise moment when friendship is formed. As in filling a vessel drop by drop, there is at last one which makes it run over; so in a series of kindnesses there is at last one which makes the heart run over.

—JAMES BOSWELL

This is one of Moody's most familiar illustrations. It's been used by other preachers since the turn of the century.

What makes the Dead Sea dead? Because it is all the time receiving, but never giving out anything. Why is it that many Christians are cold? Because they are all the time receiving, never giving out.

—DWIGHT L. MOODY

DO WHAT I CAN

If I can stop one heart from breaking
I shall not live in vain:
If I can ease one life the aching,
Or cool one pain.
Or help one fainting robin
Unto his nest again,
I shall not live in vain.

—EMILY DICKINSON

Truth 1

Kindness in words creates confidence.

—CHINESE SAYING

Kindness

Truth 2

Kindness in thinking creates profoundness.

—CHINESE SAYING

Truth 3

Kindness in giving creates love.

—CHINESE SAYING

Let us never forget that an act of kindness is in itself
an act of happiness. It is the flower of a long inner
life of joy and contentment; it tells of peaceful
hours and days on the sunniest side of the soul.

—MAURICE MAETERLINCK

Make thy study a regular thing; say little and do
much; and meet every man with kindness.

—THE TALMUD

THE PENNEY WAY

It was at a weekly sales meeting that plain speaking J. C. Penney, the dry good entrepreneur, was asked by an employee, "What do you mean, 'There's only one 24-carat rule in this company' Mr. Penney?"

The merchant lost his smile and spoke soberly to the stock boy, "That rule, my young man, is summed up in the words of Jesus Christ, 'Do unto others as you would have others do unto you.'"

"Does that mean the customer's always right?"

"No," Penney replied, his smile returning, "It means that the customer is always treated with respect and kindness, even when he's dead wrong."

Kindness is the golden chain by which
society is bound together.

—JOHANN VON GOETHE

&e

"You've always been so good to me, Dad," the
extravagant coed wrote home, "but I haven't
gotten any money from you in two months.
What kind of kindness is that?" Her father
wrote back, "Consider it unremitting kindness."

ANDROCLES AND THE LION

When Caligula was emperor of Rome, there was a young Christian slave by the name of Androcles. One day when the youth was gathering mushrooms in a forest outside of Rome, a lion came bounding into the scene. The frightened slave believed his time had come, until the beast, howling in pain, held out his paw toward Androcles. The young man saw a sharp thorn imbedded in the paw.

In a mighty surge of compassion the slave removed the thorn and then fearfully covered his face. When he opened his eyes, the lion was gone.

Years pass and Androcles huddles in the Roman circus awaiting death at the jaws of a wild beast. When a mighty lion steps into the arena, Androcles drops to his knees in prayer.

Suddenly recognizing Androcles, the great beast saunters over to the Christian and offers his paw as a gesture of appreciation for the young man's kindness in the forest. This miracle is seen by the emperor, who declares Androcles to be a Christian who knows the importance of kindness. So, both he and the lion are set free.

—ANCIENT FABLE RETOLD BY
PAUL M. MILLER

SHARING THE FRUIT OF KINDNESS

Develop the quality of gentleness, particularly toward those who are younger or weaker.

SHARING THE FRUIT OF
KINDNESS

Be aware that being kind and considerate is
more admirable than being tough and strong.

SHARING THE FRUIT OF KINDNESS

Foster the tendency to understand
rather than confront.

SHARING THE FRUIT OF KINDNESS

Go out of your way to make and keep friends.

SHARING THE FRUIT OF
KINDNESS

Make helpfulness and cheerfulness the
tenor of your life.

SHARING THE FRUIT OF KINDNESS

Take time to listen with your ears, eyes, and heart.

SHARING THE FRUIT OF KINDNESS

Give praise when it is earned.

SHARING THE FRUIT OF
KINDNESS

Genuinely forgive someone who hurts you.

SHARING THE FRUIT OF KINDNESS

Apologize for something you have done wrong.

SHARING THE FRUIT OF KINDNESS

Cultivate the habit of helping someone in need.

SHARING THE FRUIT OF KINDNESS

Give Hugs!

SHARING THE FRUIT OF KINDNESS

When conscience will allow, compromise.
Don't start a fight.

SHARING THE FRUIT OF KINDNESS

Again, when conscience will allow, negotiate.

Don't blame.

SHARING THE FRUIT OF KINDNESS

Empathize. Don't gossip.

SHARING THE FRUIT OF KINDNESS

Determine to help problem-solve.

Don't tease or name-call.

Remember, O Lᴏʀᴅ, thy tender mercies
and thy loving kindnesses.

—Pꜱᴀʟᴍ 25:6 KJV

As far as possible without surrender,
be on good terms with all persons.

—MAX EHRMANN

Take time to be friendly—It is the road to happiness.

Take time to dream—It is hitching your wagon to a star.

Take time to look around—It is too short a day to be selfish.

Take time to laugh—It is the music of the soul.

—OLD ENGLISH PRAYER

In 1982, writer Anne Herbert coined the phrase, "Practice random acts of kindness and acts of senseless beauty," which has spawned a movement to counteract random acts of violence.

As Christian believers, it is not necessary to join a Random Acts organization, but it is imperative to demonstrate the fruit of kindness.

—PAUL M. MILLER

MAKE ME A BLESSING

Make me a blessing, Make me a blessing,

Out of my life may Jesus shine;

Make me a blessing, O Savior I pray,

Make me a blessing to someone today.

—IRA B. WILSON

MARTIN OF TOURS

Tradition and Christian art have celebrated an incident in the life of a fourth-century soldier and saint, Martin of Tours, that has made him a glorious example of a Christian disciple who bore the Spirit's fruit of kindness.

On a frigid, frosty morning at the gate of Amiens, Martin, on horseback, encountered a near-naked poor man begging for alms. Seeing that those who went before him ignored the shivering man, Martin dismounted, cut his cloak in two pieces, and wrapped one of them around the frozen beggar, who clasped his arms around the soldier and wept. "My brother," Martin whispered, "take this wrap in the name of my Christ."

That night as he slept, Martin was visited by a smiling Jesus dressed in the piece of his cloak which had been wrapped around the freezing beggar at the gate of the city. Unmistakably, the soldier heard his Master say, "Because you did it to the poor man, you did it for Me."

Whether a dream or a vision, Martin of Tours has become "patron saint" of kindness and sharing.

A songwriter found inspiration in
2 Corinthians 5:14:
"Christ's Love Compels Us."

YOUR LOVE COMPELS ME

Your love compels me, Lord,
To give as You would give,
To speak as You would speak,
To live as You would live.
Your love compels me, Lord,
To see as You would see,
To serve as You would serve,
To be what You would be.

—DOUG HOLCK

Make sure that nobody pays back wrong for wrong, but always try to be kind to each other and to everyone else.

—1 THESSALONIANS 5:15

WHERE CROSS THE CROWDED
WAYS OF LIFE

Where cross the crowded ways of life,
Where sound the cries of race and clan,
Above the noise of selfish strife,
We hear Thy voice, O Son of Man!
The cup of water giv'n for Thee
still holds the freshness of Thy grace;
Yet long these multitudes to see
the sweet compassion of Thy face.
O Master from the mountainside
make haste to heal these hearts of pain;
Among these restless throngs abide.
O tread the city streets again.

—FRANK MASON NORTH

Oh Lord, help me . . .

      not only to hear your word—

            but to implement it,

    not only to love your word—

           but to live it,

    not only to profess our faith—

        but to practice it.

                —PAUL MEDFORD

Love is patient, love is kind.

—1 CORINTHIANS 13:4

Shine through me and be so in me that every soul I
show kindness to may feel your presence in my spirit.

—JOHN HENRY NEWMAN

No one needs kindness more than someone who doesn't deserve it.

—ANONYMOUS

The impersonal hand of government can never
replace the kindly hand of a neighbor.

—H U B E R T H . H U M P H R E Y

When I was young, I admired clever
people. Now that I am old, I admire kind people.

—ABRAHAM HESCHEL

Yours are the only hands
with which he can do his work. . . .

Yours are the only eyes through which his
compassion can shine upon a troubled world.

—St. Teresa of Avila

෨෬

Our natural inclination is to show kindness only to those
for whom we have some natural affinity—family, friends,
likable neighbors. But God shows kindness to those who
are most despicable—the ungrateful and wicked.

—JERRY BRIDGES

Faith of our fathers, we will love
Both friend and foe in all our strife,
And preach Thee, too, as love knows how
By kindly words and virtuous life.

—FREDERICK W. FABER

WHAT JESUS SAYS ABOUT
KINDNESS . . .

If someone strikes you on the right cheek, turn to him the other also. And if someone wants to sue you and take your tunic, let him have your cloak as well. If someone forces you to go one mile, go with him two miles.

—MATTHEW 5:39-41

WHAT JESUS SAYS ABOUT
KINDNESS . . .

Blessed are the merciful, for they will be shown mercy.

— MATTHEW 5:7

&c

WHAT JESUS SAYS ABOUT KINDNESS . . .

You are the salt of the earth. . . . You are
the light of the world.

—MATTHEW 5:13-14

❧

WHAT JESUS SAYS ABOUT KINDNESS . . .

Love your enemies, do good to them. . . . Then your reward will be great, and you will be sons of the Most High, because he is kind.

—LUKE 6:35

❧

WHAT JESUS SAYS ABOUT KINDNESS . . .

To a woman caught in the act of adultery . . .

Go now and leave your life of sin.

—JOHN 8:11

. . . And to her accusers

If any one of you is without sin, let him be the first one to throw a stone at her.

—JOHN 8:7

I WOULD BE TRUE

I would be true, for there are those who trust me;
I would be pure, for there are those who care;
I would be strong, for there is much to suffer;
I would be brave, for there is much to dare.
I would be friend of all—the foe, the friendless;
I would be giving, and forget the gift.
I would be humble, for I know my weakness;
I would look up—and laugh—and love—and live.

—HOWARD A. WALTER

❧

Be kindly affectioned one to another with
brotherly love; in honour preferring one another.

—ROMANS 12:10 KJV

AND BE KIND

Do the thing you believe in. Do the best you can in
the place where you are and be kind.

—SCOTT NEARING

Additional copies of this book
are available from your local bookstore.

OTHER TITLES FROM HONOR BOOKS:

The Fruit of the Spirit Is Love • The Fruit of the Spirit Is Joy • The Fruit of the Spirit Is Peace

If you have enjoyed this book, or if it has
impacted your life, we would like to hear from you.
Please contact us at:

Department E • P.O. Box 55388 • Tulsa, Oklahoma 74155

HONOR BOOKS
Tulsa, Oklahoma